Essentials of Long-Term Care

Steven M. Bragg

AccountingTools®

Published by AccountingTools, Inc., Centennial, Colorado.

ISBN 978-1-64221-170-2

For more information about AccountingTools® products, visit our Web site at www.accountingtools.com.

Table of Contents

About the Author

Steven Bragg, CPA, has been the chief financial officer or controller of four companies, as well as a consulting manager at Ernst & Young. He received a master's degree in finance from Bentley College, an MBA from Babson College, and a Bachelor's degree in Economics from the University of Maine. He has been a two-time president of the Colorado Mountain Club, and is an avid alpine skier, mountain biker, and certified master diver. Mr. Bragg resides in Centennial, Colorado. He has written more than 300 books and courses, including *New Controller Guidebook*, *GAAP Guidebook*, and *Payroll Management*. He has also written the science fiction novel *Under an Autumn Sun*, first book in *The Auditors* trilogy.

Steven maintains the accountingtools.com web site, which contains continuing professional education courses, the Accounting Best Practices podcast, and thousands of articles on accounting subjects.

Buy Additional AccountingTools Courses

AccountingTools offers more than 1,500 hours of CPE courses, with concentrations in accounting, auditing, finance, taxation, and ethics. Related courses that you might like include:

- Essentials of Annuities
- Essentials of Disability Insurance
- Essentials of Life Insurance
- Estate Planning Fundamentals
- Wealth Management

Go to accountingtools.com/cpe to view these additional courses.

AccountingTools®

Essentials of Long-Term Care

Introduction

It is entirely possible that you or a loved one will end up in an assisted living facility, nursing home, or some similar type of housing. This type of care is extremely expensive, and requires informed planning to ensure that you can handle the financial burden. In this manual, we cover the housing options available for those needing long-term care, as well as the available options for paying for it.

The Benefits of Preparation

Sometimes, a person becomes ill suddenly, requiring you to make an abrupt decision about where they should live. While you may not be able to anticipate the exact timing of these events, you should be able to weigh the options for long-term care well before the event. By doing so, you will have a better idea of the costs and benefits of each option, so that you can rapidly narrow down your choices when the time comes. This is especially important when your financial situation is not robust, so that you will need a good knowledge of the less care-intensive options that will not clear out your bank account.

> **Tip:** Advance planning is especially important when you may require medical care at some point in the future, since you may not be in any condition to evaluate options at the point when you need to go into long-term care.

Assess Medical Needs

One of the first preparatory steps in developing a set of long-term care options is to assess the medical needs of the person in question. If the person is currently suffering from a medical condition, consider talking to a physician about the likely development of this condition, the timing of any expected changes, and the type of care that will eventually be needed. In some cases, a medical condition may stabilize, allowing you to plan for the same level of care for an extended period of time. In other cases, an enhanced level of care will be required. This analysis may require the involvement of a geriatric specialist.

> **Tip:** Involve in your medical needs assessment someone who is in regular contact with the person in question. This individual has the best view of the person's physical and mental condition, and is best placed to advise on whether the person's current condition is representative of his or her long-term condition. Without this insight, you might end up committing to a long-term care solution that is not precisely tailored to the person's actual needs.

A result of this medical needs assessment is a general idea of the level of care required. This might, for example, initially involve at-home care that is supplemented by occasional nurse visits, followed by a transition to a residential facility that eventually leads to more intensive medical oversight.

Assess Personal Needs

Some people embrace long-term care facilities with enthusiasm, while others will do anything to stay at home. You should take their preferences into account, especially if they are capable of managing without any outside assistance, or fairly limited assistance. Remaining at home may be a clear choice in cases where there are sufficient funds to pay for a reasonable level of at-home care. Or, if they are comfortable with the services provided by a care facility, they may have a strong preference to go into such a facility sooner, rather than later. In either case, try to take their preferences into account, given the presence of any financial constraints.

Explore Family Assistance Options

Before delving into the residential care facility options, discuss within your family whether it might be possible to have a family member provide on-site care. This is a good option when the person does not require enhanced medical care, and there is someone within the family with both the time and inclination to provide services. This obligation can be massive, since the family member may make daily visits to the older person's home, cook meals, provide transportation for medical check-ups, and so forth.

A variation on the concept is for the older person to move in with family members. This can reduce the amount of time required to care for the person, and also allows the older person to sell his or her home, thereby providing cash to pay for long-term care costs. However, this option requires time and extra living space, and also prevents the family from taking time off to be on their own, perhaps for many years.

> **Tip:** These options work best when other members of the family are willing to provide supplemental assistance, either in the form of money or on-site care while the primary caregivers take time off.

Explore Family Leave Options

When discussing long-term care options, you should fully understand the amount of family leave that you are allowed under the law. You may have family leave options under the terms of the Family and Medical Leave Act (FMLA). If a company has at least 50 employees during at least 20 calendar work weeks of the current or preceding year, the FMLA allows its employees to take up to 12 unpaid weeks of leave for a variety of reasons related to family and medical issues. Key reasons supporting a leave of absence are as follows:

- The birth of a child
- Caring for a family member who has a serious illness

- Caring for an injured service member in the family
- Having a serious illness that renders the employee unable to perform his or her job

The FMLA restricts this leave of absence to those employees who:

- Have worked for the company a total of at least 12 months, including a minimum of 1,250 hours in the last 12 months.
- Work at a company facility where at least 50 of its employees work within a 75-mile radius.

> **Note:** Some states have enacted laws that make the FMLA applicable to businesses having as few as 15 employees, and have expanded the definition of a family.

If employees fall under the protection of the FMLA and take leaves of absence for the reasons allowed under the Act, the employer must continue to provide them with the medical insurance for which they had already signed up before going on leave. The company can continue to require them to pay the same employee deduction that had been in effect prior to their leave of absence. If an employee does not pay for his portion of the medical insurance within 30 days, the company is entitled to cancel the insurance for the remaining period of his leave of absence. A few additional conditions of the FMLA are:

- If the medical coverage or the terms of the employee-paid portion of the insurance are altered during a person's leave of absence, these changes will apply to the person on leave.
- If a person's medical insurance is cancelled due to non-payment, it must be restored once he returns to work.
- Only continue a person's medical insurance through a period of leave. Other benefits are not addressed by the FMLA.
- An employee must be given the same or equivalent job upon his or her return from leave.
- No seniority accrues to an employee who is on leave.
- If an employee is salaried and paid in the top ten percent of employees, and restoring this person to his or her previous position would cause "substantial and grievous economic injury," this person's job is defined as a *key position*, and the company may deny reinstatement to the individual.

EXAMPLE

Jennifer Morris works for Suture Corporation. She takes a leave of absence to care for a terminally-ill parent, which is covered under the FMLA. She had been covered under Suture's medical insurance plan prior to her leave of absence, under which she paid the company $300 per month as her portion of the expense.

While Ms. Morris is out on leave, the cost of Suture's medical insurance plan increases dramatically, causing the company to reduce benefits and increase the employee-paid portion of the cost to $500. Ms. Morris concludes that she cannot pay this increased amount, and stops paying Suture her share of the expense. Once her payment is 30 days overdue, Suture cancels her participation in the insurance plan.

The FMLA will only cover your situation if you are taking time off to care for a child, spouse, or parent. Any time off taken to care for other parties, such as a sibling or parent-in-law, is not covered by the FMLA.

Determine Financial Resources

A key element in preparing for long-term care is determining the amount of your financial resources. This assessment is primarily targeted at the financial resources of the older person for whom you are planning long-term care, but can also include any amounts that other family members are willing to contribute. The assessment should include the following areas:

- *Your estimated income, net of income taxes.* This should include Social Security benefits, disability benefits, income from any expected pensions, rental properties, businesses, and other income sources.
- *Your liquid assets.* This should include the balances in your bank accounts, certificates of deposit, money market funds, stock and bond holdings, precious metals, and so forth.
- *Your personal property.* This should include the estimated liquidation value of any antiques, works of art, jewelry, motor vehicles, the face value of whole life insurance, and interests in any businesses.
- *Your real estate.* This should include the market value of your real estate holdings, net of any mortgages outstanding.
- *Any offsetting liabilities.* This should include any debts owed to third parties. You might exclude debts owed within the family, if you believe that they will be cancelled when the long-term care situation begins.

The preceding assessment will give you a reasonably accurate idea of the funds that you can apply to a long-term care arrangement. In addition, there are several other possibilities to consider that could generate significant amounts of funds. They are as follows:

- *Accelerated death benefit.* A useful life insurance policy rider is the accelerated death benefit. This rider triggers a payout if the insured party is diagnosed with a terminal illness. A variation is the terminal benefits rider, which is designed for people with terminal illnesses; they can collect part of their life insurance early, in order to pay for their ongoing care.
- *Insurance policy cash surrender value.* Depending on the type of life insurance you have, it may be possible to cash in the policy now. The amount you receive will be significantly less than the face value of the policy, and the

amount received may be taxable. Nonetheless, this can be a good option when you have an immediate need for the cash and no other financing options.

> **Note:** Medicaid does not consider the face value of a life insurance policy to be a cash asset. However, if you cash in the policy, then Medicaid does count it as an asset. If so, and you previously had few assets, then this extra cash might put you over the Medicaid eligibility limit, so that you no longer qualify for Medicaid benefits.

- *Life settlement.* Under life settlements, terminally ill life insurance policy holders sell their policies to investors for a percent of the death benefit. To do this, the investor will need to pay an amount greater than the cash surrender value[1] of the policy (which the insured could obtain from the insurer anyways), but less than the death benefit associated with the policy. This premium over the cash surrender value is needed to convince policy holders to sell. The investor then becomes the new beneficiary of the policy, pays all remaining premiums, and eventually collects the death benefit. The intent behind these arrangements is to give the policy holders enough cash to support them through the remainder of their lives.

> **Note:** The amount received from an investor under a life settlement arrangement will be lower if you are relatively young and healthy, since the investor cannot expect to receive a death benefit for a long time. Conversely, if you are older and in poor health, the investor can expect a more rapid payout of death benefits, and so will be willing to pay more to take over your policy.

- *Reverse mortgage.* This is a type of home loan that allows homeowners aged 62 or older to borrow money against the equity in their home. They do not make any monthly payments while they are living in the home. The loan will be repaid when the borrower sells the home or dies. This is a good option for someone who wants to use a home health care option. However, the closing costs associated with these loans can be high, while the related interest cost compounds over time. The result can be very little residual equity to be passed on to heirs.

Once you have explored these options, you will have a clear idea of the older person's medical issues, the ability of family members to render assistance, and the likely amount of financial resources that will be available to support the person's long-term care. The next steps are to find someone to assist you in evaluating available resources, and to then explore the types and costs of those resources.

---

[1] Cash surrender value is the cash value stated on a life insurance policy, minus any surrender charge and any outstanding loans and interest.

Find a Geriatric Care Manager

Once you have completed the preceding assessment, you will be in a good position to decide upon the best long-term care options. However, what if you do not have the time to review them yourself, and especially if you are living in another part of the country? If so, consider hiring a geriatric care manager. These people provide guidance on the available care options, and can manage the process on your behalf. They may have a personal knowledge of specific facilities, and so are in a good position to make a selection on your behalf that meets both your long-term care needs and your budget. In particular, they may have a good knowledge of local facilities that specialize in treating people who are suffering from Alzheimer's disease. That being said, you should still visit any recommended care locations to see if they meet your requirements; it is possible that you will change your instructions to a geriatric care manager once you have seen a selection of recommended properties.

It can be difficult to determine whether a care manager will be the right person to provide you with assistance. It is better to work with one who has deep experience in the field, perhaps having worked in a care facility in the past. You should also check the person's references and job history. In addition, obtain their pricing structure up front, so that you can estimate how much will be charged for an initial assessment and ongoing work on your behalf. It is also useful to discuss whether the care manager can work with you on extremely short notice, in case the older person needs to move into a long-term care facility right away.

Tip: Inquire as to whether a geriatric care manager has a business arrangement with any long-term care facilities that pays them a commission for referrals. If so, you may end up paying substantially more for a long-term placement than would otherwise have been the case.

If you cannot afford to use a geriatric care manager, other options are to consult with any friends who have already dealt with long-term care situations, your physician's office, the local senior center, or the social services administrator at the local hospital.

The Range of Long-Term Care Options

If family assistance is not an option, then you will need to explore the many types of long-term care options that may be available in your area. It makes sense to have a general overview of the types of care that may be available to your specific circumstances. The classes of care are noted in the following exhibit.

Long-Term Care Options

Type of Care	Cost[2]	Features
Adult day care	Low	Provides socializing events, exercise, and meals at local facilities. Designed for those who live at home or with family members.
Assisted living	Medium to expensive	A private or shared room in a residential facility with all meals provided, as well as some personal care and housekeeping assistance.
Combination residential facility	Medium to expensive	A facility that offers varying degrees of assistance, from independent living to nursing facility care, depending on each person's needs.
Home care	Medium	An arrangement where a senior lives at home, with a variety of services provided by parties that visit the home to prepare meals, do housekeeping, and so forth.
Home health care	Medium to expensive	This is a more enhanced level of service than home care, where nursing assistance and/or physical therapy is also provided. Usually associated with a recovery from an injury or illness.
Hospice care	Low	This is care provided at home for those with terminal illnesses. The focus is on pain relief and keeping the person comfortable. The cost is rated as low, since it is mostly paid for by Medicare.
Independent living	Medium to expensive	Residential facilities for seniors that have on-site facilities and services. It does not provide any personal services or health care, and so is intended for reasonably independent seniors.
Intermediate care nursing facility	Expensive	This facility provides a reasonable level of medical care, and is intended for those with disabilities or long-term illnesses. Can be used for short-term care, until a person moves to a different type of facility.
Long-term care facility	Expensive	This facility provides basic levels of assistance, health monitoring, nursing care, meals, and housekeeping for those with permanent or long-term injuries or illnesses.
Personal care facility	Medium	A room in a long-term care facility with all meals provided, as well as some personal care and housekeeping assistance. May be a private home.
Respite care	Low	This is on-site care by a temporary worker, which is intended to give family members some time off from their assistance duties.
Skilled nursing facility	Expensive	This facility provides constant oversight, nursing care and physical therapy, along with all personal assistance needed. It is usually limited to short-duration stays following an injury or illness.

---

[2] Generally, the cost to stay at a facility is lowest in smaller facilities, since they are more likely to be privately-owned and have fewer staff. Larger facilities are more expensive, because they tend to be better-equipped and have larger staffs. This does not mean that the best service is provided by the largest facilities – only that a greater expenditure has been made on assets that seniors may not even use.

> **Tip:** Before selecting any one of the preceding long-term care options, find out whether it is subject to inspection by a state agency. If so, contact the applicable agency and review its most recent inspection report on the facility.

The options noted in the preceding exhibit occupy a broad swathe of monthly costs. Generally, occasional home care is the least expensive option, but it can transition into the most expensive option of all if you want 24/7 home care. In terms of a residential facility, independent living facilities are the least expensive option, though this depends on their location and the quality of the facilities provided. Assisted living facilities are more expensive, and will escalate rapidly in price if the person requires extensive medical oversight. We explore these options in greater detail in the following sub-sections (which are listed in alphabetical order).

Adult Day Care

This service is provided from a central facility, where the staff monitors seniors and provides both meals and activities to them. The intent is to provide some social care in a group setting for those who are still living at home. Adult day care is inexpensive, and so is a good way to reduce the cost of in-home care for a few hours per day. However, most of these organizations provide few medical services to seniors, which restricts this option to those who are in reasonably good health.

A few adult day care centers *do* provide a modest level of medical services, such as health testing and administering medications. This requires better staff training, so the cost of these centers will be higher. The associated benefit is that those seniors who are not in reasonably good health can still attend these facilities.

Adult day care centers typically offer half-day or full-day programs, for which attendance is scheduled in advance. Some of these facilities also offer transportation, which can reduce the burden for family members who are caring for seniors.

Assisted Living

An assisted living facility starts with the services available to seniors through an independent living facility, and layers on the services provided by on-site nurses. Under this arrangement, seniors live in rented apartments that have additional safety features, such as bathroom handrails, emergency call buttons, and even hospital beds. In addition, they receive constant monitoring, as well as personal assistance that covers housekeeping, meals (usually all three meals, every day), and hands-on assistance with tasks that they are no longer able to perform on their own. These tasks may include dressing, eating, bathing, getting out of bed, using the toilet, and so forth. The level of aid offered is not continuous; instead, a staff person might (for example) assist a resident in getting out of bed each morning, plus one or two visits during the day, and render assistance in going back to bed at night.

> **Tip:** Review the contract with an assisted living facility to determine exactly which services will be provided, and how frequently. Also, see if the facility will allow you to take meals in your room, rather than in the common dining room.

In addition, an assisted living facility usually has a nurse on the premises who can provide referrals for medical care, keep track of medical appointments, and ensure that residents take the drugs that have been prescribed for them.

The best assisted living facilities provide extensive social activities for residents. This may include lectures, exercise classes, games, and opportunities for residents to gather. These activities are usually posted within the facility.

There are a few concerns associated with assisted living facilities. One is the frequency with which the facility may raise the rent. Assisted living facilities owned by larger corporations have a well-earned reputation for raising rates to maximize their profits. Another issue is that facility rules may force you to leave once your age exceeds a maximum threshold value, such as 85 years old. They may also force you out if you require an excessive level of assistance that calls for more than a few staff visits per day.

Tip: It is possible that you may have an illness that forces you into the hospital for an extended stay. If so, the facility may hold your room for a short period of time, after which it may offer you priority to re-enter it over new applicants. Check the rental agreement to see if this option is provided; otherwise, an extended hospital stay may result in you having to make new living arrangements.

Despite these concerns, assisted living is a good approach for those seniors who are no longer able to live entirely on their own, but who do not want to (or cannot) go into a more expensive nursing home, which may cost twice as much. This can also be a temporary solution for someone who is suffering from the early stages of dementia, but who will eventually require more intensive oversight in a nursing home.

Combination Residential Facility

A combination residential facility is a larger long-term care facility that incorporates a range of options for residents. It offers independent living, as well as more intensive assistance and nursing arrangements. These facilities are designed to provide services to seniors for many years, as they gradually require more assistance. Transfers between the various units of the facility will depend on availability, so it may be necessary to wait for a unit to open up.

A variation on the concept is for the facility to offer seamless transfers to different levels of care whenever residents need it. However, this approach means that the facility must keep some units open to meet demand, which increases the fees that it must charge to residents. It may offer residents a *life care contract*, under which it guarantees (for steep initial and ongoing fees) all levels of care that residents may require for the rest of their lives. A variation on the life care concept is a contract that guarantees your access to nursing care for a fixed number of days per year, after which your costs will increase.

> **Tip:** If you are considering a life care contract, then fully inspect the facilities for assisted living and full-time nursing care, to see if they measure up to your expectations. Many seniors only inspect the independent living part of these facilities, on the assumption that they may never need the other facilities. In addition, check the contract terms to see if you can receive a refund of your initial fee if you subsequently elect to leave the facility.

There are several advantages to moving into a combination residential facility. First, seniors can settle into a comfortable environment over a number of years, and one which offers roughly the same routine. They will also have the same group of neighbors for many years, and likely many of the same staff over that period of time.

Home Health Care

One of the least expensive long-term care options (depending on the circumstances) is home health care. Under this option, an older person can continue to live at home for an extended period of time, usually with a variety of support services being provided by outside parties. This approach works well when an older person is reasonably mobile and does not require constant medical monitoring. The support services that may be provided include the following:

- General companionship
- Housekeeping and home repairs
- Meal delivery[3], meal planning, or on-site meal preparation
- Medical alert service, where seniors wear a device that allows them to contact an emergency response service simply by pressing a button
- Medical and safety equipment, including beds, wheelchairs, and oxygen equipment
- Nursing assistance (under the oversight of a physician) with diagnostic monitoring, injections, intravenous medication, and similar matters
- Physical and speech therapy assistance
- Personal assistance, such as assistance with moving around, taking a walk, bathing, toilet needs, and getting dressed[4]
- Telephone reassurance service, where someone calls each day to serve as a safety check
- Transportation services

These services may be provided by a mix of service organizations, community service centers, friends, and family. When paid service providers are providing some or all of

---

[3] Meals on Wheels is a low-cost meal delivery service that is available in many communities; it usually delivers a hot lunchtime meal to those who have signed up for the service.

[4] Personal assistance in a home health care environment is especially useful when a person is suffering from dementia, because the care person is providing one-on-one assistance, and so is in the best position to monitor the person on a continuing basis.

the services, be sure to examine their fee schedules. They may have a minimum fee per visit, as well as higher rates for evening or weekend work.

> **Tip:** Home health care is one of the more complex long-term care undertakings, so prepare a written plan for who will provide which services, and for what periods of time. This plan may require frequent updates, depending on the changing condition of the person for whom care is being provided.

A key advantage of home care is giving a person a sense of control over his or her environment by being able to live independently. Also, you will be in a better position to refine exactly what types of care are being provided, especially if a family member checks in regularly to observe and discuss matters. In addition, you can avoid paying the substantial fees charged by senior residential facilities.

The main downside of home care is that outside services are not usually able to provide services on a continual basis, so you will still need to have a family member living in the vicinity who can monitor the situation on a regular basis. In addition, this person will need to be involved frequently, to manage the various care providers. A further concern is that an older person is more likely to feel isolated at home, as opposed to the companionship commonly associated with a well-organized senior residential facility. And finally, you may experience some discontinuity in care, as a variety of care providers come and go, depending on their individual circumstances.

> **Tip:** If you plan to use one or more independent aides to care for an older person, be aware that these people may have their own emergencies or become sick, and so may not be available – and with very little notice. To guard against this, always have a backup person available who can fill in on short notice.

> **Tip:** When evaluating a home health care option, be sure to factor in the cost of having a family member drive to the home on a regular basis, as well as the cost of that person's time – both in transit and on-site. These costs can be substantial.

Home health care may not last for an extended period of time, especially if an older person is suffering from a degenerative disease that will eventually require more intensive care. Consequently, it makes sense to anticipate how long you can maintain a home health care situation, and what will be the next logical long-term care option.

> **Tip:** While there are highly professional organizations that can provide very high-quality home health care services, this may come at a high cost. Depending on your financial circumstances, it may make more sense to obtain services merely from the most adequate provider – it all depends on the situation. That being said, a full-service agency may be your best bet if no family members are located nearby, since an agency is best placed to coordinate support.

Hospice Care

Hospice care is provided at home for those with terminal illnesses. Many seniors opt for hospice care, rather than continually shuttling between a nursing facility and a hospital, and back again as they deal with increasingly numerous bouts of illnesses. There may be no benefit to this cycle, so seniors instead elect to switch over into hospice care, which can enhance their quality of life. Under a hospice care arrangement, the focus is on pain relief and keeping the person comfortable for the remainder of his or her life, and typically involves a substantial amount of assistance from nurses, aides, and volunteers.

Hospice care can be conducted anywhere, including a person's home. Under this arrangement, you are monitored regularly and administered with whatever medications are needed to make you comfortable; there is no attempt to treat the underlying disease. There is a hospice physician who sets up your treatment plan, and nurses will be available to monitor it and administer medications as needed. There may also be therapists who will assist you in maintaining your mobility in order to go about the necessities of daily life. There are no attempts to enhance your mobility.

The cost of hospice care is low, since it is mostly paid for by Medicare, on the grounds that it is much less expensive than maintaining someone at a long-term care facility. In addition, most medications are provided directly by the hospice program, as is any medical equipment (such as a hospital bed) and medical supplies that you may require. Consequently, this is an excellent choice for those within what will likely be the final six months of their lives.

> **Note:** Hospice care is provided for an initial 90-day period, after which your physician reviews your situation and decides whether you should stay in the program. If you are continued in the program, the physician will conduct another evaluation in 90 days. After that, the evaluations occur at 60-day intervals.

Independent Living

A good option for those seniors not in need of medical services is independent living. These facilities provide socialization options for seniors who want to live together and who are able to take care of themselves, without imposing the high costs associated with nursing assistance. These facilities are usually equipped with extensive safety options, such as handrails, ramps, elevators, and good lighting. They may also have a number of commercial services on-site, such as a workout area designed for seniors, dining rooms, laundry services, and a beauty salon.

The more extensive assisted living services provide a continuum of care, where basic living needs can be provided at lower cost, with more intensive services also available for an additional fee. However, units that provide more intensive services may not be available when needed, which forces some residents to look elsewhere when they need additional assistance.

There are a broad range of facilities that fall under the category of assisted living. Some are quite luxurious, with refined features, a golf course, tennis facilities, and other recreational options. There are midrange options set up as clusters of condominium units, and there are much more basic facilities that are essentially renovated older rental units that feature few amenities.

> **Note:** If you are not quite able to live on your own, some assisted living facilities will provide you with outside assistance options for such services as housecleaning and meal preparation.

There are some downsides to assisted living facilities. They may require seniors to move out once they exceed a certain maximum age, in effect forcing them into more expensive facilities. For example, a facility might require you to leave once you reach 85 years of age.

Another downside is that a facility may force you out if you are not able to maintain a minimum level of physical capability. For example, some facilities do not allow residents to use walkers, and/or to eat without assistance in the dining area. Or, they may force you out if you become fully incontinent.

> **Note:** A potential concern for couples moving into an independent living arrangement is what happens when one of them is no longer physically able to live there. Will the facility's rules force out both of them, or can the disabled senior continue to remain there if being assisted by his or her more capable companion? Be sure to check the rules.

Another concern, which depends on the quality of the services being provided, is that some assisted living facilities can be quite expensive – especially since they tend to be staffed at a higher level than standard living arrangements for younger people. The expenses associated with independent living can include the following:

- *Entrance fee.* An entrance fee can be substantial, and may not be refundable when you eventually move out. Alternatively, the amount that can be refunded may decline over time.
- *Monthly maintenance fee.* There may be no restrictions on the frequency with which monthly maintenance fees increase.
- *Additional services fees.* The facility may charge extra for a variety of services, including transportation, laundry, workout facilities, and additional meals.

Some independent living facilities offer an inclusive contract, under which the ongoing facility fee covers all of the services provided; this is useful if you plan to live on-site most of the time and participate extensively in the facility's offerings.

> **Tip:** Watch out for situations in which an independent living facility has recently been purchased by a larger business. The acquirer will likely want to generate a return on its investment, and so can be expected to increase fees in the near future, possibly combined with a cost-cutting campaign that will negatively impact the quality of services being provided to residents.

Another downside to independent living is that these facilities usually operate under a number of rules, such as the time periods during which meals are offered, and the modifications that residents are allowed to make to their units. These rules are needed in order to efficiently operate the facilities and maintain a consistent standard of living for residents, but some seniors can find them to be irksome.

Note: For those seniors of limited means, it may be possible to obtain housing that has been subsidized by the government. These facilities can be substantially less expensive, but also provide lower-quality services.

Tip: When investigating an independent living facility, ask to see its record of rent increases for the last few years. If these increases have been substantial, it is likely that the landlord will continue to impose large rate increases in the future.

In cases where an independent living facility requires you to purchase a unit, there may be restrictions on later selling it. These restrictions mandate that the buyer also meet the facility's standards for physical mobility and age. The facility may also reserve the right to buy back the unit, which could force you into a sale for less than the market value of the property. It is also quite likely that rules will prevent you from renting out your unit. Given these restrictions, it makes sense to read the purchase agreement thoroughly prior to buying a unit, perhaps with the assistance of an attorney.

Nursing Facility

A nursing facility generally provides a significantly higher level of nursing care along with on-site residency and all meals, typically better than what can be obtained from any other type of facility. Within this category, a facility at the low end may provide only low levels of nursing assistance (called custodial care), while a facility at the high end provides both constant and intensive care (called skilled nursing care). A custodial care facility may provide assistance for an extended period of time, while a skilled nursing care facility will likely do so for a much shorter period of time (given its extremely high cost), typically following an illness or injury.

Nursing facilities are the penultimate form of long-term care, in that they provide the most intensive level of care to seniors. However, they are also both expensive and difficult to get into, due to a high level of demand. Consequently, it makes sense to start reviewing nursing facility options as soon as you think you might need to enter one, and be willing to do so as soon as space becomes available. Otherwise, you might have to wait for an extended period of time to do so after your physical condition has deteriorated.

Tip: Before moving into a nursing facility of any kind, check to see if it is Medicaid-certified. If so, Medicaid will pay for your stay in the facility, as long as you qualify for Medicaid. This certification ensures that the facility meets the health and safety standards set by the Medicaid program.

Respite Care

Respite care involves the use of scheduled companions for short periods of time during the day, so that family members providing care can have some time off. Those providing respite care are generally not trained nurses, and fulfill a monitoring and companionship role more than anything else. Some respite care can be provided by volunteers, in which case there is no cost associated with it.

Care Requirements for Those with Alzheimer's Disease

Alzheimer's disease is the most common cause of dementia, which is the loss of memory and other cognitive abilities that is serious enough to interfere with a person's daily life. This disease accounts for somewhere in the range of 6% to 80% of all dementia cases. It is a progressive disease, where the symptoms gradually worsen over a number of years. Memory loss is mild in its early stages, gradually becoming much more severe. The average person with Alzheimer's will live anywhere from four to ten years after being diagnosed, though some patients may live for as long as 20 years.

During the early stages of Alzheimer's, it is possible for a patient to stay at home under observation, which may require the family to hire personal care givers who supplement the oversight of family members. However, during the mid-stages of Alzheimer's it will be necessary to shift the person to a residential care facility. Also, if there are few family members in the vicinity who can provide at-home assistance, then this shift to a facility will have to occur earlier.

> **Tip:** If you plan to keep an Alzheimer's patient at home, then refit the home to minimize the dangers to that person. This means locking off dangerous areas of the home (such as the basement), locking away sharp objects, installing night lights, and adding motion sensor alarms to warn you when the person is moving around at night.

> **Tip:** For at-home care, try to find aides with prior Alzheimer's experience, since this type of care requires a great deal of patience, as well as a soothing personality that can settle people who are continually confused and troubled.

In cases where one person in a couple has Alzheimer's, a reasonable solution for a few years is for both to move into an independent living facility, so that the workload of the healthy person is minimized, allowing him or her to take care of the sick spouse. A further advantage of this arrangement is that independent living facilities are relatively small, allowing for a reduction in housekeeping requirements. Yet another advantage is that other seniors living nearby can keep an eye out for the sick spouse, in case the person attempts to wander away.

Eventually, it will be more likely that the person will require constant oversight in a skilled nursing facility, where all medical services are provided around the clock. Many of these facilities have established specialized units that focus on treating Alzheimer's patients, with specially-trained employees. In some cases, they may only accept Alzheimer's patients, which means that their entire staffs are experienced in dealing with Alzheimer's symptoms. However, this care is quite expensive, so family members will usually try to hold off on this solution for as long as possible. Conversely, paying for on-site care can be even *more* expensive, where you are paying for someone to be at your house for three shifts, all year long. Such intensive care is actually more expensive than the cost of a skilled nursing facility, which may drive the decision regarding what needs to be done.

Tip: Discuss with the facility administrator its policy regarding the use of antipsychotic drugs. These are heavily used to keep Alzheimer's patients under control, but the over-medication of patients does occur. Discuss who decides whether these drugs will be administered, the dosages given, and their frequency. You may want to discuss this policy with your family physician to get a second opinion on whether it is reasonable.

Facility Selection Considerations

There are a number of issues to consider when selecting a specific facility for long-term care. Besides the obvious issue of cost, here are several other issues:

- *Activities*. Does the facility offer a variety of activities to its residents, such as on-site lectures or outings to shopping facilities, the library, or a park?
- *Ambiance*. Is the facility a pleasant one in which to reside, or is it old, drafty, not well-maintained, and so forth? This is a particular concern when you are expecting quite a long-term arrangement.
- *Complaint procedure*. Does the facility have a well-defined process for handling complaints by residents and family members? Is there a clearly-identified person who is responsible for dealing with complaints?
- *Condition of other residents*. Walk around the facility to see what the other residents are doing. Are they left alone in the corridor, or do they appear happy and are engaging in conversations? How clean and well-dressed do they appear to be? These are strong indicators of how well the facility is run.
- *Counseling*. Is there an on-site counselor who can provide referrals to outside agencies, or assistance with any financial issues you may have?
- *Employees*. Are there enough aides to provide support to residents within a reasonable period of time? The number of aides will vary greatly, depending on the type of facility. In addition, does there appear to be a great deal of staff turnover? If so, this is a sign of low pay and high stress, which may be reflected in the attitude of aides towards the residents. In addition, watch the staff as they interact with residents to see if they are friendly and courteous.
- *Facility location*. Consider picking a facility that is easy to get to, and which has a variety of nearby options for taking a resident on an outing.
- *Family notifications*. Does the facility give adequate notice to family members when a resident is going to be moved to a new room, including an explanation of why the change is being made?

- *Food.* If the facility serves meals, visit the dining area and determine whether the food being served is reasonably tasty, whether a choice of meals is offered, and whether snacks are available during non-meal hours. In addition, take a hard look at the dining area, to see if it is comfortable and clean.
- *Healthfulness.* A facility should not have any odors that indicate a lack of cleaning. It should also be sufficiently large to not feel cramped, and be equipped with all necessary safety features.
- *Hospitalization policy.* It is quite common for residents to be sent to a nearby hospital for periods that may be extended. When this happens, what is the facility's policy for re-admitting the resident?
- *Medication control.* How well does the facility keep track of resident medications, and whether residents are taking their medications as prescribed?
- *Medication fees.* Depending on the type of facility, there may be a requirement for residents to purchase all medications from the in-house pharmacy – which can have substantial markups attached to them.
- *Personal care.* Does the facility offer on-site personal care, such as haircuts and clothes washing?
- *Private rooms.* Are there private rooms, or are residents forced to share space with others? How large are these rooms, and are they structured to provide some degree of privacy?
- *Public areas.* A facility should have a sufficient number of public areas where residents can relax and socialize. A variation is a quiet room, where residents can get away from the others and sit quietly. There should also be outside areas where residents can spend time in the fresh air.
- *Rules.* What are the facility rules for watching a television in your room, or for accepting visits, or for dealing with excessively noisy roommates? Also, how flexible are its rules in regard to meal times, visiting hours, and bringing in aides for additional assistance?
- *Safety.* How safe is the surrounding area? While it is unlikely that residents will be harmed (if they never leave the facility), this could be a concern for visitors.
- *Security.* Is there a safe designated for each resident, where valuables can be stored?
- *Size.* Is it too large? A massive facility may feel overly institutional. Conversely, a small facility with just a few residents might present a better opportunity for socializing with a few immediate neighbors.
- *Temperature control.* Can residents control the temperature in their rooms?
- *Third party guarantor.* A facility should not require other parties to guarantee the payment of its fees. This can heap a large liability onto people who cannot afford it. Instead, the arrangement should restrict the liability to the assets of the resident.
- *Visiting areas.* Are there adequate visiting areas where friends and family can visit? Are they large enough to handle everyone who wants to visit?

Many of the preceding points will not be obvious if you only conduct a brief visit (which is the case for many family members who are in a rush to place an elderly relative). Despite the difficulty involved, it makes sense to check the reviews for a facility, and any issues noted by state inspectors.

Tip: Use the preceding facility selection considerations to create a checklist for the issues that matter the most to you, and use it to evaluate each of the facilities that you visit. This is a good way to conduct an apples-to-apples comparison of the facilities.

Medicare Long-Term Care Benefits

Medicare is a health insurance program for people age 65 and older, and people under 65 with certain disabilities. It consists of four programs, which are as follows:

- *Hospital Insurance (Part A).* This covers some of the costs associated with a hospital stay or a skilled nursing facility.
- *Supplementary Medical Insurance (Part B).* This pays some of the costs of physicians and outpatient care.
- *Medicare Advantage (Part C).* This is a private health plan that is approved by Medicare, and which offers an alternative to Original Medicare. MA plans typically include Part A (Hospital Insurance), Part B (Medical Insurance), and usually Part D (Medicare prescription drug coverage).
- *Medicare Prescription Drug Benefit (Part D).* This is a voluntary program that helps Medicare beneficiaries pay for outpatient prescription drugs. It is offered through private health insurance companies that contract with the federal government.

Medicare is incorrectly considered to cover a large part of the costs of your long-term care. Medicare will cover the cost of a skilled nursing facility for up to 100 days of continual treatment (minus a co-insurance charge), but that is all. Also, if you no longer require skilled care in such a facility within that 100-day period, then Medicare will no longer pay for it. Further, it does not cover the cost of most types of residential care, including assisted living and long-term nursing facilities.

Medicare also covers some of the costs of skilled nursing being provided to you in a home health care setting, as well as reasonable therapy costs, and certain types of medical supplies and medical equipment. In this environment, it does not cover meals, housekeeping costs, prescription drugs, or any personal care being provided by aides. Even these limited benefits are only granted when you are homebound, have a doctor certification regarding your status, and the agency providing care is certified by Medicare. If you qualify, then the provider must accept full payment from Medicare – it cannot charge additional amounts to you.

Medicare covers the cost of hospice care under Medicare Part A. In addition, you must give up all medical interventions to cure or at least delay your decline due to the underlying illness (though you can later elect to reverse this decision and exit hospice care), and formally enroll in a hospice program. This does not mean that you have to give up all medical interventions – only the ones related to your terminal illness. Accepting Medicare coverage of your hospice care also means that you will only be able to use a Medicare-approved hospice program, though you can still work with your primary care physician to treat other conditions.

> **Tip:** Some families do not want to believe that a loved one only has six months (or less) to live, but this certification by a physician is a good way for the family to cut costs substantially through Medicare coverage of hospice care. So, if you can accept this prognosis, the financial benefits are substantial.

> **Tip:** It is advisable to continue paying for your Medicare Advantage plan or Medigap supplemental insurance[5] while receiving hospice care, in case you subsequently exit the hospice program and return to the regular Medicare program.

Medicaid Long-Term Care Benefits

Medicaid is a federally-funded insurance program that is administered by the individual state governments, and which provides free or low-cost health coverage to some low-income people, families and children, pregnant women, the elderly, and people with disabilities. Many state governments have expanded the coverage of their Medicaid programs to cover all people below a certain income level; this has resulted in substantial differences in eligibility limits, depending on the state in which you reside. In addition, some states charge a small enrollment fee, co-payments, and a monthly premium.

Medicaid covers the cost of long-term care in a nursing facility[6] for an indefinite period of time, but only for those people who fall within its low-income threshold, and who have few personal assets (with some exemptions). For many people, this means that you must pay for long-term care out of your own assets until they are nearly gone, after which you can access Medicaid benefits. Even then, most of your monthly income will go to the facility (with some allowances excluded), with Medicaid paying for the remainder of your care fees. In addition, Medicaid will seek reimbursement from your estate after you die, up to the amount it paid your bills.

> **Note:** Medicaid pays a lower rate for a room in a long-term care facility than is charged to those paying privately. This means that a number of care facilities do not accept Medicaid-funded residents, or put them in lower-quality rooms. A possible outcome is that, if you start off in a facility for which you are personally making payments and later switch to Medicaid, you might find yourself being shunted off into lesser accommodations. Also, if the facility does not participate in the Medicaid program, then it can force you to find accommodations elsewhere.

---

[5] Medigap insurance is private insurance that fills in some of the gaps in your Medicare coverage.

[6] Medicaid does *not* pay for your room and board in an assisted living facility.

In addition to its coverage of the care provided at nursing facilities, Medicaid also provides benefits in other areas, which are as follows:

- *Hospice care.* Medicaid covers the cost of hospice care, and does so under the same requirements stated earlier for Medicare.
- *Home care services.* Medicaid covers most of the cost of home care, which includes housekeeping, personal care, and respite care. The range of services provided varies by state, as does the percentage of the cost of care that Medicaid covers.
- *Home health services.* Medicaid covers the cost of nursing care and aides who come to your house, as well as various forms of therapy. However, the number of hours of this coverage (or the number of visits) is limited.

A common ploy by many seniors is to give away their assets to relatives in order to drop under the minimum asset threshold required by the Medicaid program. This is difficult to do, since you will be required to fill out many forms when you apply for Medicaid coverage that ask you to itemize your assets. Medicaid will also review your personal transactions for the preceding five years to see if you have disposed of any assets, which can result in penalties[7], fines, and the denial of coverage.

The basic rule for giving away assets (which depends on the state in which you apply for coverage) is that you can only have done so more than five years prior to your Medicaid application. There are stringent exceptions that allow asset transfers within this look-back period. The primary exception is that you can transfer title to your home to your spouse, as long as the spouse continues to live in it. Another option, though perhaps an emotionally difficult one, is for you to divorce your spouse, thereby shifting assets to your spouse in a manner that Medicaid cannot pursue. Such a divorce needs to show that the two of you are leading separate lives, which means that your housing, bank accounts, and other assets are separately owned. Before pursuing any of these changes, you should discuss your options with an attorney who is knowledgeable in regard to the Medicaid rules in your state.

Veterans Long-Term Care Benefits

The Department of Veterans Affairs (VA) offers some long-term care to veterans. The main benefit types are as follows:

- *Direct care.* The VA operates a number of nursing homes and other residential facilities, and also provides for long-term care in your home. It contracts with private nursing homes when it does not have any available facilities within a geographic region. It also operates community living centers that can accommodate veterans for short periods of time with a variety of conditions

---

[7] The penalty is a delay in when you will qualify for Medicaid that corresponds to the amount of money that you gave away during a state-specific look-back period. The more money you gave away during this period, the longer you will have to wait to qualify for Medicaid.

– and which also provide hospice care. Qualifying for direct care will depend on your financial situation, the existence of a disability, and your physical condition.

- *Home care*. The VA can provide nursing assistance in your home, as well as some personal care services, hospice care, and transport to local VA facilities for additional assistance. Co-payment amounts may apply, depending on the situation.
- *Direct payments*. If you have a service-connected disability, then you might receive monthly disability payments, based on a disability rating. If you are housebound, you may receive an additional payment. The VA also issues a monthly pension payment to low-income veterans under certain conditions, which can be increased if you are housebound.

Long-Term Care Insurance

As noted earlier in this manual, there are many holes in the long-term care coverage provided by government programs. If anything, the default condition is that you will have to foot the bill yourself. And, given the extreme expense of some forms of long-term care, it is quite likely that you will face a financial strain when the time comes. One way to address this looming liability is to obtain long-term care insurance.

As the name implies, long-term care insurance will pay for some or all of your long-term care, but only under very specific circumstances. Insurers need to restrict the conditions under which payouts occur, because the payouts can be extremely expensive for them. For example, the insurer might not pay for the cost of home aides, respite care, hospice care, or care at local day care centers. These restrictions are imposed in order to drive down the cost of the insurance, but also restrict the circumstances under which it might be of use to you.

Given the high costs of long-term care even for the restricted conditions under which you will qualify for benefits, the cost of the insurance is very high[8]. Consequently, you will need to decide whether your physical condition makes it more probable that such a policy will be cost-effective for you. When making this decision, here are some of the issues to consider:

- *Inflation risk*. The cost of long-term care will go up at the rate of inflation or faster. Therefore, any insurance policy that does not provide for inflationary increases in care costs is not a good deal. Instead, only investigate the cost of those policies that take the impact of inflation into account. This may simply reflect the annual cost of living increase in your area, or a policy may increase the payout percentage based on a compounded rate (so that the annual inflation increase is based on the payout for the immediately preceding year). The

---

[8] An insurer will probably conduct a physical examination when you apply for long-term care insurance, and may deny coverage or charge you a very high premium if it believes that you will need lots of long-term care. In short, if you need it, you can't get it – and if you don't need it, you *can* get it.

latter option is obviously better, since it increases your eventual payouts, but will also require more expensive premiums.

Note: Some policies cap the number of years over which inflation protection is applied. Therefore, if you are applying for this insurance at a relatively young age, be sure to obtain the longest possible inflation coverage period, so that you will be protected when you need it.

- *Medicaid probability.* If your income and assets are so low that you will likely qualify for Medicaid, then don't waste your money on a long-term care policy; you will already be covered by Medicaid.
- *Premium affordability.* Most long-term care insurance claims are made by people who are more than eighty years old, which means that – on average – you will be paying for this insurance for a long time before there is any prospect of actually using it, including after you have retired and are not in as good a position to afford it. A better option might be to invest the money yourself, so that you will have a cash reserve whenever you actually need long-term care.
- *Your sweet spot age.* The best age at which to enter into a long-term care insurance contract is when you are in your fifties or sixties. Before this point, the premiums will be lower, but you will still be paying a substantial amount for a long time. After this sweet spot, it is more likely that your application for coverage will be denied; in addition, the premiums will be extremely high.

When deciding whether to enter into a long-term care insurance contract, it can be quite useful to model a variety of scenarios, and see if this option makes sense for you. For example:

- You enter into the insurance contract at age 60, pay $500 per month for 20 years, and then die, never having made a claim. In this case, you have lost $120,000 with no offsetting benefit.
- You enter into the same contract at age 60 and pay the same amount for 20 years, and then enter a nursing home, where the policy pays out $200 per day for a maximum of four years. This represents a payback of $292,000 to be balanced against your total payments of $120,000, which represents quite a reasonable return.

The preceding scenarios represent the opposite extremes of possible payout scenarios. The most likely outcome is probably somewhere in between, where the insurer has structured the contract terms to reduce the probability of any payouts being made. For example, the insurer will likely include a requirement that you be incapacitated for at least 90 days before any benefits will be paid; this clause is intended to avoid payouts in situations where you are recovering from an illness or injury over a relatively short period of time, which covers most care situations.

The best long-term care insurance pays you a fixed indemnity amount per day, rather than using any number of restrictions to cap the types of expenditures that you can make. Thus, it is better to receive a daily payment of $250 and decide for yourself how to spend it, rather than arguing over (for example) whether someone qualifies as a certified home health care professional, and then paying a percentage of that person's wages.

A key element of a long-term care policy is the policy definition of what will trigger benefits. The policy typically states that the triggering event occurs when you are unable to perform certain activities of daily living, which cover such items as eating, dressing, using the toilet, walking, and so forth. When you need assistance with a certain number of the activities on this list, the policy will be activated. Clearly, you will want a policy that requires a smaller number of these triggering events (such as two), rather than one that requires your almost complete immobility before it begins paying out.

Be aware that many long-term care policies exclude coverage if your underlying condition is based on a chemical dependency, alcoholism, mental illness, or a self-inflicted injury. If you are already suffering from one of these conditions, there is not much point in applying for the insurance, since you might pay premiums for years – and then be denied coverage.

As you age, it may become financially more difficult for you to keep paying premiums. If so, consider looking for a policy that makes some provision for this situation. One option is a waiver of premiums, where you no longer have to pay a premium once you begin collecting benefits. Or, look for a step-down provision that allows you to scale back the benefits to be paid out in exchange for a lower premium. And, for cases in which you are completely unable to continue paying premiums, look for a policy that allows you to collect either reduced benefits or benefits for a shorter period of time, once you have paid premiums for a certain minimum number of years.

Tip: Insist that your own doctor certify you as being unable to perform activities of daily living, rather than a doctor appointed by the insurer.

Tip: If a proposed policy's coverage period is two years or less and the daily coverage cap is under $100, it is probably not worthwhile to obtain the insurance at all. Conversely, coverage that extends beyond five years may be so expensive that it is also not worthwhile, especially when balanced against how long you will probably live in a nursing home.

Tip: If you decide to purchase a long-term care insurance policy, be sure to apply to several insurers. The reason is that they all have different underwriting methodologies, so some of them will charge you a lower monthly premium than others, even while paying out the same benefits.

> **Tip:** If you are relatively young when you enter into a long-term care insurance contract, consider having the insurer insert a payment cap into your policy – perhaps for 20, 25, or 30 years from now. Doing so will give you full coverage, and eliminates a monthly expense (the insurance premium) during your retirement.

A variation on the long-term care concept is one that has a built-in whole life insurance component. Under a whole life policy, you pay a fixed premium payment on an ongoing basis. The residual cash value of the policy increases over its term, though the cash value is quite low over the first few years of the policy; this is because the agent's commission can easily be half of the first-year premium, if not more. This policy contains a provision that it will pay for your long-term care up to a certain maximum amount, with any residual payout being paid to your beneficiaries upon your death.

These hybrid whole life – long-term care policies might initially seem interesting, since they also provide for a payout to your beneficiaries. However, the overall return on these policies tends to be rather low, since they pay out a significant commission to the insurance agent and have ongoing administrative costs. Consequently, it is usually more economical to simply invest your money and use the proceeds to pay for your own long-term care.

> **Tip:** If you already have a life insurance policy, you might sell it for a percentage of the death benefit. The buyer then becomes the new beneficiary of the policy, pays all remaining premiums, and eventually collects the death benefit. The intent behind these arrangements is to give you enough cash to support you through the remainder of your life.

If (despite the concerns expressed here) you still decide to purchase long-term care insurance, at least spend lots of time investigating the exact wording of the contract that the insurer wants you to sign, to ensure that it contains the features that you want. Pay particular attention to any wording that limits the amount of long-term care payments made, as well as wording that allows the insurer to increase your insurance premiums. In addition, consider investigating the insurer's financial stability. The more stable insurers maintain high levels of liquidity, and so are better able to honor their contractual obligations. The best way to ascertain financial strength is to obtain an insurer's financial strength rating. The ratings are provided by four primary rating agencies, which are A.M. Best, Standard & Poor's, Moody's, and Fitch Ratings. Each of these agencies uses its own rating system to devise a ranking for an insurer. A comparison of their rating systems appears in the following exhibit.

Comparative Insurer Rating Systems

A. M. Best	Standard & Poor's	Moody's	Fitch Ratings
A++ Superior	**AAA** Extremely Strong	**Aaa** Exceptional	**AAA** Exceptionally Strong
A+ Superior	**AA+** Very Strong	**Aa1** Excellent	**AA+** Very Strong
A Excellent	**AA** Very Strong	**Aa2** Excellent	**AA** Very Strong
A- Excellent	**AA-** Very Strong	**Aa3** Excellent	**AA-** Very Strong
B++ Good	**A+** Strong	**A1** Good	**A+** Strong
B+ Good	**A** Strong	**A2** Good	**A** Strong
B Fair	**A-** Strong	**A3** Good	**A-** Strong
B- Fair	**BBB+** Good	**Baa1** Adequate	**BBB+** Good
C++ Marginal	**BBB** Good	**Baa2** Adequate	**BBB** Good
C+ Marginal	**BBB-** Good	**Baa3** Adequate	**BBB-** Good
C Weak	**BB+** Marginal	**Ba1** Questionable	**BB+** Moderately Weak
C- Weak	**BB** Marginal	**Ba2** Questionable	**BB** Moderately Weak
D Poor	**BB-** Marginal	**Ba3** Questionable	**BB-** Moderately Weak
E Under Regulatory Supervision	**B+** Weak	**B1** Poor	**B+** Weak
F In Liquidation	**B** Weak	**B2** Poor	**B** Weak
	B- Weak	**B3** Poor	**B-** Weak
	CCC+ Very Weak	**Caa1** Very Poor	**CCC+** Very Weak
	CCC Very Weak	**Caa2** Very Poor	**CCC** Very Weak
	CCC- Very Weak	**Caa3** Very Poor	**CCC-** Very Weak
	CC Extremely Weak	**Ca** Extremely Poor	**CC** Extremely Weak
		C Lowest	**C** Distressed

In addition to these financial ratings, consider researching the complaints filed against an insurer to see if any of them are unusually aggressive in contesting claims, or take a long time to begin paying claimants. This information should be available through your state's department of insurance, though a general Web search may also reveal pockets of complaint information on other sites.

It is possible that your employer or trade association will offer you the option to purchase group long-term care insurance. Under these arrangements, the insurer or trade association offers a standard contract to all employees or members. The following exhibit outlines the differences between these options.

Comparison of Long-Term Care Insurance Policy Types

	Individually-Purchased Policy	Group Policy Purchased through an Association	Group Policy Purchased through Your Employer
Summary	This is a policy that you purchase yourself, through an insurance agent	This is a policy that you purchase yourself, through an association of which you are a member	This is a policy that your employer provides; either you or your employer pays the premiums, or split the bill
Policy conditions	You must meet the underwriting criteria imposed by the insurer	You must be a member of the association	You must be an employee of the business
Policy advantages	You select the amount and type of policy benefits, and any benefits are tax-free	Underwriting requirements may be fairly loose, but acceptance is not guaranteed	You usually do not have to meet any underwriting criteria
Policy disadvantages	This is the most expensive option	Tends to be a less flexible policy design, and may restrict benefits or the conditions that qualify you for long-term care	Tends to be a less flexible policy design, may restrict benefits or the conditions that qualify you for long-term care, and may change your premiums and/or benefits if you leave the employer

You should have a clear understanding of exactly what types of long-term care a policy will cover. While individual policies may have terms that differ from what is stated here, most policies will provide coverage for the costs of home care, assisted living, nursing facility care, and hospice care. Some policies will charge a higher premium for some of these types of care. Your main focus should be on whether a policy covers the cost of nursing facility care, since this is the most expensive type of care.

Legal Matters

It is possible that you will have physical or mental problems prior to your death that will render you incompetent to make certain decisions. If so, several arrangements can be made to ensure that you are taken care of during any period of personal incapacity. We cover these options in the following pages.

Planning for Personal Incapacity

One way to deal with personal incapacity issues is to not plan for them at all. If so, and you later become incapacitated, then a judge will appoint a guardian to make decisions on your behalf. This approach is not recommended, since the associated court time is expensive, as are the ongoing fees charged by the guardian – which can cut substantially into your estate. In addition, anything stated during court proceedings will generally be public knowledge, which may not be a desirable state of affairs.

A better option is to set up legally valid documents that direct how your affairs should be handled in the event of your incapacitation. For example, you can specify what medical actions are to be taken in the event of an injury or medical condition. In particular, you can specify whether you want to receive life-prolonging treatments when the resulting quality of life will be low, or whether these treatments are to be withheld. In addition, you can specify who is authorized to make these decisions. Further, you can specify who will handle your finances, and provide this person with direction regarding how assets are to be invested and what expenditures to authorize. This person can deal with such matters as using your assets to pay for ongoing expenses, pay taxes, invest excess funds, manage your retirement accounts, and so forth.

> **Note:** If you can communicate your wishes in any way, then any legal documents concerning medical or financial decisions are not activated. They are only activated when you are in a permanent coma.

Planning for personal incapacity is especially important when the members of your family have differing opinions about what to do. To avoid rifts within the family over these decisions, take the matter away from them by preparing legally valid controlling documents.

Health Care Directives

In most states, you should prepare two documents that allow you to specify the nature of your medical care, both of which are classified as health care directives. The first is a declaration (also known as a *living will*), which is intended for medical personnel, and which identifies the medical care that you want to receive, as well as the medical care you do *not* want to receive in the event of your incapacitation. This document is targeted at whether you want to receive expensive and possibly painful treatments that may only prolong your life for a short period of time. Medical personnel should either follow your directive or transfer you to someone who will do so.

> **Note:** Be sure to state in your living will whether you want to receive pain medication, since a directive to stop such medication could leave you in significant discomfort during a final illness.

In addition, you should create a durable power of attorney for health care, in which you designate someone to act on your behalf to ensure that medical personnel are giving you the medical care that you specified. This person may also be authorized to have a relatively broad authority to make decisions concerning the types of health care that you will receive. For example, this person might have the power to give or withhold consent for certain medical procedures, hire or fire medical personnel, and obtain court authorizations when medical providers do not want to honor your wishes.

Note: A do-not-resuscitate order states that you do not wish to be revived if your heart stops or you stop breathing. It must usually be signed by a doctor to be considered valid. It is also known as a DNR form or DNR directive. The form should be kept in an obvious location where emergency medical personnel can see it, such as on the front of your refrigerator.

EXAMPLE

Jeffrey has been ill for quite a long time, and now faces a major surgery that will likely incapacitate him for an extended period. He creates a durable power of attorney for health care, in which he delegates to his sister Dorothy the power to make medical decisions on his behalf. Jeffrey includes several conditions in this document, including a requirement that all surgery be conducted at Saint Mark's Hospital, with Dr. Anderson performing the surgery.

Depending on the state, health care directives are generally not valid until you sign them in the presence of witnesses, which may include a notary public. This requirement is needed in order to prove that you were of sound mind when you created the documents.

Tip: Review your health care directives every few years, to ensure that you agree with the wishes codified in the documents. If not, replace them with new versions. To make this replacement easier, maintain a listing of who has received copies of these documents, so that their copies can be destroyed and replaced with the new versions.

A durable power of attorney for finances is used when you want a trusted person to take over your financial affairs while you are incapacitated. This document can be designed to take effect immediately, or only after a doctor certifies that you have been incapacitated. In the first case, the document goes into effect as soon as you sign it. In the second case, the document is known as a *springing power of attorney*, and only goes into effect when a party stated in the document decides that you are now incapacitated; this can involve obtaining a doctor's statement regarding your incapacity. A springing power of attorney document can be difficult to construct, so have an attorney write it for you.

A durable power of attorney should be signed in the presence of a notary public, and possibly other witnesses (depending on state law). Otherwise, your agent may have difficulty getting third parties to accept him or her as your valid agent. Keep this document in a safe place where your agent can access it, since the document will be needed to obtain the cooperation of financial institutions.

Note: If a durable power of attorney for finances gives your agent power over real estate, then it must be filed in the land records office of the county in which your property is located.

Your Health Care Agent

The selection of a health care agent is a difficult one, for you are imposing a hard task on another person – deciding whether to give you certain types of medical care, which in turn may result in your death. This can be an especially troublesome task when there are multiple medical options to sort through, where the outcomes are not certain. The following points are worth considering when making the selection:

- Does the person live nearby? If so, it will be easier for the person to regularly travel to the hospital to monitor your condition.
- Does the person have enough fortitude to follow through with your wishes? This is a particular concern when some family members have alternative opinions about your treatment.
- Does the person have a reasonable knowledge of the medical procedures that might be involved? When this is the case, the agent will be able to compare the available options and make the best choice that matches your stated wishes.

Tip: Designate a backup agent, in case the primary agent is unable to serve.

It can make sense to give your power of attorney for financial matters to the same person who will be your health care agent. Otherwise, you may end up with two people who have difficulty working together to manage your affairs.

Tip: Unless your financial affairs are quite simple, it is generally prudent to allow the person handling your finances to receive a reasonable amount of compensation for his or her efforts on your behalf.

The capstone to planning for your personal incapacity is making sure that all health care directives are already in the hands of your doctor, agent, and at least one other party. Having these documents well distributed in advance limits the risk that no one will be able to find the documents when you are incapacitated.

Summary

The key underlying issue associated with the planning for long-term care is to start evaluating the situation and your options well in advance – preferably multiple years in advance. This initial planning will be based on your health condition at that time, and will likely require updating in subsequent years, as your health gradually changes. By taking this approach, you can involve family members in the process and set expectations for who will be involved in your care, your preferences for long-term care, and how the associated expenses will be handled.

Glossary

A

Accelerated death benefit. A life insurance policy rider that triggers a payout if the insured party is diagnosed with a terminal illness.

Assisted living. Housing for elderly or disabled people that provides nursing care, housekeeping, and prepared meals as needed.

C

Cash surrender value. The cash value stated on a life insurance policy, minus any surrender charge and any outstanding loans and interest.

F

Family and Medical Leave Act. An Act that entitles eligible employees to take unpaid, job-protected leave for certain family and medical reasons with continuation of group health insurance coverage under the same terms and conditions as though the employee had not taken leave.

H

Home health care. When an older person can continue to live at home for an extended period of time, usually with a variety of support services being provided by outside parties.

Hospice care. Care that is provided at home for those with terminal illnesses, where the focus is on paid relief and keeping patients comfortable.

L

Life settlement. The sale of an existing life insurance policy to a third party in exchange for cash. The third party eventually collects on the payout from the policy.

Living will. A legal document that states a person's preferences for medical treatment if they are unable to make their own decisions due to a terminal illness or being unconscious.

R

Respite care. The use of scheduled companions for short periods of time during the day, so that family members providing care can have some time off.

Reverse mortgage. A type of home loan that allows older homeowners to borrow against the equity in their home.

S

Springing power of attorney. A document that only takes effect when specific conditions are met, rather than immediately after it's signed.

Index

www.ingramcontent.com/pod-product-compliance
Lightning Source LLC
Chambersburg PA
CBHW051429200326
41520CB00023B/7407